LENI'S *TRIUMPH*

OTHER BOOKS BY COLIN FALCK

Poetry collections

Post-Modern Love
Memorabilia
Backwards into the Smoke

Literary criticism

Myth, Truth, and Literature: Towards a True Post-Modernism
American and British Verse in the Twentieth Century: The Poetry that
Matters

Edited works

Robinson Jeffers: Selected Poems
Edna St Vincent Millay: Selected Poems

LENI'S *TRIUMPH*

AND OTHER POEMS

COLIN FALCK

Shoestring Press

Printed by imprintdigital
Upton Pyne, Exeter
www.digital.imprint.co.uk

Typesetting by narrator
www.narrator.me.uk
info@narrator.me.uk
033 022 300 39

Published by Shoestring Press
19 Devonshire Avenue, Beeston, Nottingham, NG9 1BS
(0115) 925 1827
www.shoestringpress.co.uk

First published 2020
© Copyright: Colin Falck
© Cover image: Still from 'Triumph des Willens' reproduced with permission from Bundesarchiv / Transit Film GmbH

The moral right of the author has been asserted.

ISBN 978-1-912524-54-9

ACKNOWLEDGEMENTS

My exceptional thanks are due to Damon Falck, without whose massive electronic help this book would not exist.

My special thanks are due to Anthony Astbury and Greville Press for publishing many of these poems in the pamphlet *Beating Retreat* (2018).

My thanks are due to the editors of the following magazines who previously accepted some of these poems for publication: *Agenda, Ambit, London Magazine, The London Review of Books, The Rialto, The Spectator, Swansea Review* and *The Times Literary Supplement*.

I am grateful to James Greene, David Harsent, Declan Ryan, Robert Stein and Hugo Williams for their many and varied kinds of advice and help over many years.

To
my family: Sonja, Damon and Lawrence
with all the love I'm capable of

Also to
Hugo Williams

Backward through grasses

CONTENTS

MESSAGE

In south east London, in the first years of the war,
in a houseless dead-end street, set back from a back-street,
a street where dogs would copulate and a few kids played,
there was this low brick building with a permanently-closed
    garage door.
Scratched into the door's paintwork, in its lower-right corner,
was a swastika with a deep-scored message: HITLER IS IN HERE.
We guessed it wasn't really true, but we would play quite near.

Not-quite-remembering that withdrawn grey-paint façade
you turned a familiar corner six decades later:
there, old-dirt-begrimed, with an England flag on a van,
was that lost-world garage, now part of a run-down builders' yard.
If you bent down and squinted hard into the evening light,
your face against the blistered paintwork, it would faintly appear:
the old, unsuperseded message: HITLER IS IN HERE.

I

MODEL VILLAGE

It's more like a country town. Go in through the gate:
there's a waterfall, some slums, a coal-mine, a factory or two,
some sheep farms, a Grand Hotel, a lake with a pier.
Fifty by seventy yards (your path winds through),
you're caught in a microcosm. What's been laid out here
is a June afternoon in 1938.

It's a rambling stretch of ground, just one small hill
with a windmill on it. You can walk all round—admire
the railway; the horse carts; the period shops and cars;
the scouts and guides; the thatched roof always on fire;
the gypsies; the pubs (saloon and public bars);
the theatre where Gracie Fields once topped the bill.

The sun shines down, and—still bemused by the Olympics—
everyone seems to be doing outdoor sports:
there's track and field; two judges peer at a clock;
cyclists ride round in baggy, decent shorts;
some long-dressed ladies play bowls. Outside The Cock,
eight Morris dancers bang each other's sticks.

Far-off, past the rail yards, three biplanes taxi on grass.
There's a crowd. Is this Amy Johnson, back from Penang,
landed at the wrong airfield? (she was hopeless with maps).
It's not; and the rumours subside. There's a lumbering clang
from the colliery (the Saturday shift). Some lank-haired chaps
race their Jags up the High Street, and out to the by-pass.

Fortress'd from Europe, the "scept'red isle" drifts on—
tuned to its Empire. In a tiny kitchen with a wireless
(where perhaps the voice of the Führer can be heard)
a man reads his paper. There's news of crime, or Wallis,
or thunderstorms. The ladies at bowls are undeterred.
They're living off funds from their husbands, dead and gone.

The tall church steeple sounds its "triples" chime.
A bride and her chinless groom beguile their friends.
Who are these people? (you're thankful not to be there).
The last march fades. The bandstand's concert ends.
(The King.) The flags hang free in the English air.
The windmill is still. It looks like peace in our time.

LENI'S *TRIUMPH*

1. Early Leni

"The most beautiful woman in Europe," said her first director
(besotted). He wrote a script for her in three days—gave her a
    starring role
in *The Holy Mountain* ("For the dancer Leni Riefenstahl").
The film-crew and half the actors are soon in love with her.

She throws herself into the part. As "Diótima," she dances
by the sea at dawn, for the rich in a decadent hotel.
With silent-film grandeurs she lords it—not very well—
and skis. Two pipe-smoking men make shy advances

but die in the mountains. Immensities, light and shadow,
high rock-ledges, sun and snow. An allegory of the Earth:
transcendent powers dreamed up by Novalis or Wordsworth—
the redeeming purity of the mountains, the sordidness of the low.

By *The White Hell of Piz Palü* she has sealed her fame:
has worked with Pabst, can act, is on track to go far—
has all of movies before her, will be a world-wide star.
Two mountain-films later, the talkies have changed the game.

Her Berlin accent no help, her English suspect,
unable to sing like Dietrich, she is feeling the stress—
seems doomed to be a "mountain-heroine." For this high-
    climbing actress
there is nowhere upwards to go. She will have to direct.

2. Leni's *Blue Light*

Full moon, an unearthly shadow-light: a new and "impossible"
combination of filters; hauled cameras; long ropes. Another
    mountain film—
stark prayers to the weather—but this time different. Junta/Leni
(writer, actress, director) has found her perfect role. Child-waif-
    girl, witch-girl,
scorned by her village, she shares the slopes above
with sheep-flocks, carrion crows, a shepherd-boy, waterfalls, rocks,
fast-changing seasons, wild beasts; each full moon free
to climb, deft hand over hand, these cliff-face crags
to escape the world and attain the mountain's crest—
entranced, knowing her way like a sleepwalker (the papacy was
    impressed),
to repose in her crystal cave with its blue light.
Here waits all purity, all perfection, a young girl's dream.

Such hard-won beauty tests spirits, finds failure, makes victims,
    breaks hearts, costs lives
(the young men who would trail her fall to their deaths).
She graces the mountainside, husbands her loneliness, lives out
    her fate. If she could only
shine like her cave-crystals, blind with their holy perfectness;
    find a way
to disclose the mystery; bring word from these towering heights
of their healing force; reveal their power of selfless love
to the valley-benighted village and the world.

One day with swastikas, drummings, rituals, torchlight, flags—
high priestess answering a call from above—she would.

3. Leni's *Triumph*

The boxy, millennial music swirls and lurches.
Through rolling banks of cloud, sure of its way,
the Führer's plane descends—over half-glimpsed views
of bell-towers, alleyways, rooftops, tall-spired churches,
the ancient (now Adolf-Hitler-Platz) market square.
Morning in misty Nuremberg: the longed-for day.
The black Mercedes glides through ecstatic streets;
a cat on a window-sill wakens; the city's statues
turn for the cameras. Nature, ancestral lore
will be folded into this myth. To the cutting-room floor
go doubts, hesitations, obstructions, the small defeats,
the Führer nervous and worrying about his hair.

The day has the feel of mysteries that have come to birth,
of untold tales to be told. But we have seen it before.
This is time-worn history: Caesar and Caesar's legions
gathering to test the limits of the known earth.
These eagles, standards, marchings, flags unfurled
are stirrings of age-old powers—and will lead to more.
The Triumphs of Caesar will follow; and to fuel their blaze
these women in costumes, contingents from all regions,
generals, workers (unions to the fire consigned),
party subordinates, wastrels yearning to find
new lives, an end to hard luck, have converged to praise
the unmistakeable dawning of a new world.

That it did not happen, that we lived their twelve years through
and were mostly spared, is not what we should learn from this.
Behind the sixteen cameras, controlling it all,
one-time bit player, in charge at thirty-two
—a free woman, her long-shots ready to declare
for Weimar's dying liberties this grainy nemesis:
triumphant, certain, dreadful—marshalling our fears,
was star-struck Leni, happy with nothing small,
serving her god-like leader. Leni—who has made
from half-a-million feet of film, one six-day parade,
images that could haunt us for a thousand years.
Wired-in worship: what has really always been there.

4. Lift

"Now comes that incredible, indelible scene in the vast Luitpold
Arena… The little lift can be seen in some of the shots."
– Audrey Salkeld, *A Portrait of Leni Riefenstahl*

61 minutes into *Triumph* the world stops. Three far-off figures
march away from us, one slightly ahead, at a measured pace
through their ordered ranks of followers. The angle reverses
and they approach: we see their faces. To terminally beautiful music
they come near us, mount steps, stride as though all goes well,
halt with precision; salute with relaxed control
at a fire-crowned memorial to war. To all war, any war.
The smoke of forgotten holocausts drifts on the air.

Ite, missa est. The pall of enchantment lingers.
They turn and descend: all the deep-wrought spells are in place
for a thousand years of perfection. Our long-held-to defences
yield to the powers of centuries-ancient magic.
Only the busying lift with its cramped nacelle
insect-tiny on its 50-metre oriflamme pole
glides up and down, chronicling submission's score.
Leni at work: hard-won long-shots: our world still there.

5. Leni's *Olympia*

Grand festival of flags and anthems. Berlin: 1936.
The Italians, the Austrians, the French, the Turks, the Greeks
are perfecting their Nazi salutes. Two crowd-filled weeks
of wrought-up thrills and long-clamped-down emotion.
The flame from Olympia, contestants from every nation:
triumphs of strength and will, fierce soul-searching time,
the breaking of limits. For Leni, the Alpine climb
to her unreachable blue light: artistic perfection.
Cranes, tracking shots, close-ups, back-lighting, slow-motion:
black-and-white tragedy; shadows, in sharp relief.
A perfect beetle crawls nimbly over a fallen leaf.
Great art must leave our weighed-down world behind.

Long hours of "*Fertig!*" and gunshot: the *agon* unfolds—
quick camera-shy limberings, close-ups of muscles, or feet,
the high-curving discus, fresh warfare in every heat,
the power of the black athletes, the record-book leaps.
The free-style swimmers storm on to their last breath:
von Wangenheim slips at the water-jump, falls from his horse,
breaks his collar-bone—rides on and finishes the course:
the marathon runners outlast their hours with death.
The final nightfall. Enchantment; the stadium weeps.
The hymn rises up—the closing ceremony's crown.
More flags. A cathedral of light; the flame goes down.
The Führer is pleased: the world's reports are kind.
Huge dismantlings, and the city re-orders. Elsewhere,
Autobahnen are being urgently planned, false books are being burned,

the unfit perfectly sterilized, statistics returned
on employment, culture programmes, munitions, Jewish lies.
"Politics is the highest art."—We must remove the diseased,
find freedom for the healthy, make space for resurgent days:
the East will be colonized, our settlements will bring new ways.
Mankind is what is true and right—the sub-human erased.
In a new Greek order Plato might have found wise
there will be Strength through Joy, nutrition brought from afar,

lecture-trips, cruises for workers, a people's car.
The new millennium is being beaten out and refined.

Past all the miraculous editing, one image compels.
In a great triple dissolve-out, a regiment of women
fills out the screen (Beijing will do this again):
gymnastic patternings as far as the camera sees.
On a planet-sized sports field they sway to primal powers,
stare into distance, wield clubs, gyrate and swirl,
yield themselves to dreams and Providence; each girl
a guardian of the future race. Tomorrow will be ours.
Their bodies streamlined, their arms wafting like anemones,
they move in a mesmeric rhythm: timelessly at one
with nature, the life-force, tides, the moon, the sun.
Beauty: ecstasy: oblivion. The death of the mind.

6. The Gypsies

Plucked from internment, they prepare for a brighter day.
Young men, grandmothers, exotic dark-eyed children,
hand-picked for melodrama, there to perform for "Aunt Leni."
All-disposing, attentive, childless,
she beguiles them with sweets and promises, praises their ardour—
enslaved to their beauty, to their uncomplaining quickness to
learn. Gypsy-figured, though too old now, she will take the
    leading part.

She will flaunt herself, dance, watch in awe at the final knife-
    fight. They
must prowl and stare, try out poses, repine or threaten,
embody the strangeness she yearns for, be quiet or inflammatory.
They are stand-ins for all dreams of untamed life, all undefiledness,
all truth; but by the philosophies of *Heimat* and *Rasse*
consigned elsewhere. Only twenty out of more than a hundred
    who leave here will return.
The obsessiveness of the artist. The inhuman indifference of art.

7. There

The warriors in Riefenstahl's Africa photos
are on the look-out for their neighbours, keep their knives
    well-shone
but are at peace with their own kind.
Undiminished still, undismayed by the camera, they do not scare.
They glower and wave their spears
as though accusing us of their extinction.

Driven out now these thirty years
they have left bare rock-plains behind. Their old lands gone
they have taken refuge in our minds.
In books, on walls, in exhibitions
they wrestle with each other, titivate their warpaint
and stare into our lives. Their fierce eyes shine.

We do not hear their complaints.
We make brave plans for our future; have moved on,
are swept along by our new century. We leave all darkness behind,
find bright algorithms, smoother hair styles, count up our
    anniversaries, look at art books, dine,
enjoy the fruits of civilization. We draw to our close.
They are still there.

8. Leni's Defence

In 1993 an award-winning documentary
shows Riefenstahl in a pink raincoat, on guard but matronly,
re-facing the old questions: what things she has seen
and when, who else might have seen them; places she has been—
when Poland collapsed, when the gypsies slaved on *Tiefland*,
when the bombs fell… Weathering it out; or, with relief,
locked in her editing-room, reviewing for the thousandth time
the wheeling formations of *Triumph*. Name dragged through slime,
a nation's scapegoat—feared memory from their Nazi spree,
unanswered voice of their guilt (her films still banned)—
she stands by her German life; who by the end could film only
a dying African tribe, some fish on a reef.

"So what am I guilty of?", she asks.—And might have gone on:
Would it be better to have pleaded youth, ambition, like Karajan?
Owned up a bit, like Speer—done jail, become a "Nazi celebrity"?
Owned up to what?—that I knew them, that Goebbels didn't
        hate me,
that they helped with some bills, that I once had a villa in Dahlem?
I killed no one, walked over no bodies, was uninformed of
        their plots,
kept clear of the Party, had no part in the sub-human ending.
I used the world when it helped me: the invitations, the grand
        spending,
the privileges, the camera-crews, the men—they would let me be,
and I loved them, was even a wife; I did all my work with them.
All these years were my jail: fifty lawsuits; four trials; career gone.
(I lived on bread and cheese and water for my hardest shots.)

So history conspires with the victors, takes the rulers' part:
has no time for Leni, girl of the mountains, of the unbroken heart,
who would never make a film indoors; who went on being there,
surviving, scuba-diving at ninety, unfazed, unaware;
who yearned for the truth of Africa—for the primal scene
of life on this earth, of bloodshed; who reshaped its sign
for a world that had lost its way; for Leni, who could rage
at a misplaced camera; who would upbraid us girlishly in old age:

"I want to see, that's all. This is my life. I want to see";
  who emblazoned a century; whose best defence might have been:
  He was my leader, I worshipped him. He compelled me to
      make art.
You have your own madnesses now; you should leave me to mine.

(*Leni Riefenstahl, 22 August 1902–8 September 2003*)

THE PHONEY WAR

The sirens going off at 12, and all of us called in.
(Taking our trikes in to save them from getting bombed.)
Worse-than-usual Sunday dinner (fish pie, with leeks);
tea with the MacIntyre-Gibsons, all brushed and combed,
the grown-ups saying it couldn't last more than six weeks.
Mowgli at bedtime. Never hearing the All Clear.

Battleships for Christmas. Not much happening for a year
(gas-masks, rationing, Dunkirk). Then Spitfires, and the Blitz:
black-outs, some neighbours vanished, two uniformed uncles;
the Astoria Dance-Hall flattened by "direct hits";
nights in the coal-cellar, the droning Dorniers and Heinkels—
then out on the streets for bits of shrapnel next day.

A year in Devon (no visits). "Out of harm's way"—
but back in time to take control of the war.
Lord Haw-Haw ("Jairmany calling") at 7 a.m.,
maps in the paper of Voronezh, Stalingrad, Warsaw,
the Western advances; the last defeat at Arnhem;
parades and parties; my aunt's Rita Hayworth hair.

School; adolescence; sex. (Some surprises there.)
Wapshot Officer Cadet School; the war in Korea
stopping before you got there; showing off your handgun;
patrolling the Empire; not getting gonorrhea;
three Chinese girls to die for, but killing no one;
an hour (refuelling) on the tarmac at Da Nang.

Fast-forward several decades. "Life," with a bang—
Successes; Failures; career-watching; staying alive;
buying our son his trike; some unhappy families
("each in their fashion"); the Nazis on Channel Five.
D-Day: the beach-heads. The notched-up anniversaries.
Still waiting for the war to end—or begin.

DEVON

The red earth of Devon was escape from wartime London:
fresh fields to embolden a seven-year-old's change of skills—
from shape-seeking clay to iron of the far south-west.
Strange people, brown cows, longer evenings, no black-outs,
    more sun,
clear vision—even though (and as any child's drawing will attest)
there are no horizons in Devon, only lump-backed hills.

At Gravelings School, near Sheepscombe, we were taught to lead
(regardless of where); there were leaders wherever we went.
They told us about Pearl Harbor, and "the rules of war,"
and to half-look-ahead to the next words while you read.
A time-saving trick—but citified, and pursued too far
meant the whole of life missed out on, your time never spent.

Perhaps this was why at football Mr Coombes could forget—
while teaching us to chase, back-heel, pin down an opponent,
to tack and swerve with near-to-post-modernist flair—
that the aim of the game was to put the ball in the net.
The goal is no place to address the problems of "being there."
To speak is sometimes much easier than remaining silent.

The ladies who ran it were wiser; had missed out on most things
but held themselves finely: conveyed that life was hard,
took practice; that to learn to garden, write poems, cross-stitch,
was the only reckoning there was: that such slow-turned strivings
gave point to the days; might hold back the darkness.

                                    For which,
late-blooming thanks to Miss Harkness and Miss Goddard.

HOME

"Why aren't you in school then?" they'd ask—as we ran to play,
or went roller-skating, or collected caterpillars—or got started in
on the summer's work of dams, or of blowing-up wasps'-nests
(some carbide, some water—throw a match, get out of the way)
or of building Messerschmidts. Our exams were done. It was June.
There were things we needed to do, and it was time to begin.

A pulsating aerial drone... We looked up, and they were there:
Dakotas, with their Horsa gliders, three to each plane,
spaced out across the sky—as black as bats
like the silhouettes in our thumb-grimed *War in the Air.*
They were locked in a strict formation, and heading south.
The invasion!!!... (and a reason not to be in school—again).

Or at home. We ran off, to the car-park, or the market-square,
or the barbed-wired fields where the Italians slaved all day.
They were crying, and telling stories, and wiping their eyes:
"Come-a 'ere-a boys! We go 'ome-a soon!...—We see you there!"
They embraced, and laughed, and sang opera ("Un bel di..."")
and gave us sweets through their fence—while the guards
        looked away.

For hours—so it seemed—the slow June dusk wore on.
Bats now, real ones; then more planes—and still they came:
another, and another wave. We watched in the darkness,
and stayed out late till the last faint sounds had gone.
We kept the sweets. They were labeled "Gioia d'Italia."
The war had come home now; "home" would never be the same.

TEN

1. To Jennifer

A bee-filled summer—in our teacher's garden,
aged ten. Watching the pale-green branches burn.
It was "Saturday Latin," but we were allowed to see the tree-cutting
from our fairy-tale bank of ferns.

I think this was when I first learned
that all things might vanish, the declensions blur
in wood-smoke, but it would still be all right if you held hands
with a girl called Jennifer.

The house is demolished now; the teacher too.
The harsh unjointing was the best thing for the tree.
Who was it you decided to be, then?—and did it work?
The other Jennifers were a disappointment to me.

2. Transit

August, a post-war afternoon, our week "away".
The old LMS tank-engine (D-class second series, 3601)wheezes
against the buffers at Aylesbury. The Petersons are here to
    meet us
and everything feels perfect in the hazy sun.

We have chuffed here slowly, past rust-stained signal-gantries,
there were speed-limits (old flying-bomb damage) along the line,
two stations were boarded-up, a carriage was "taken out of service"
but we are here, and the engine has been fine.

It will not be with us for much longer.
Its funnel is too tall, its brasswork too fanciful and curled,
its grandfatherly air of hesitating and taking a long time over things
not right for this world.

The future will come and the past will pass. Aged ten,
you can see that there's nothing you'll be able to do.
Best just to toughen up and be moving on, then.
You will need to roll up your life behind you as you go.

3. Moving On

The main thing was to keep your head down, take no chances.
Feign obedience, know the rules, be in the right place but invisible.
Routines aside (bed squared off, wait your turn for biscuits, shoes
    properly tied)
you were expected to pay attention, laugh at the right times, and
    avoid being "wet."
As Mr Hayward explained, you didn't want to let the school
    down, or do things you might later regret
or disappoint your parents. Or—worst of all?—be like Burnside
    who cried the first week and got sent to the prep school.

There were the usual mitigating circumstances:
your own home-brought food (share with friends) to alleviate the
    school meals;
being read to (Kipling, Rider Haggard, *Tarka the Otter*) at week-
    ends in the dorm;
Mrs Wetherbee the Matron asking you to tea and remembering
    who you were.
Or film nights: Olivier's *Henry V*, *The Song of Ceylon*, *Sanders of
    the River*—
or Riefenstahl's Olympics (shown all over again to the fifth
form)—the Führer's showpiece and Mr Etherington's hymn to
    Greek ideals.

No point now in remembering the small injustices:
being snubbed by the school porter; three years of persecution
    in the gym; not being properly promoted in the Cadet Force;
getting banned from the Debating Club for making too much noise.
Unnoticed-as-yet, not much visited, aged ten, you had to make
    of it what you could
when Mr Etherington was to be seen chain-smoking over his
    books in Shelley's Wood
(and was later dismissed for his behaviour towards small boys).
Everything must be much better now, of course.

THE CALL

A false sense of calm. The distracted weeks go by.
A small brown envelope comes—you half-know what you will find:
Report to Camp Yellingfield on Thursday 20th July
at 15:30, leaving your life behind.
No luggage: slow train to West Dumpton: near-death for being late.
You're early; you've found a seat. One loud whistle-blast
and you're off—to your half-feared rendezvous with Fate.
Sit back, read your paper, watch the built-on shires go past.

Uncalled-for beauty assails you at every turn.
This is England, your home land—a land you have scarcely seen
but will soon be leaving—for where? Unrestrained now, will
    you learn
of "life under different skies", what a "killing zone" can mean,
how the world works, *who you are*, what your next few years will
    be about…?

We shuffle off at West Dumpton. They begin to shout.

NAAFI BREAK

"Will you GET a FUCKING HOLD OF IT [your rifle], *soldier!!! …*
You look like a virgin holding her first cock!!!"
Borne on the depraved rantings of the sergeant-major
you're off, down the narrow service road, past the Admin block,

twenty times round the square; then up Breakneck Hill
and back, at the double, for bren-gun training, or kitchen chores,
or floor-scrubbing; in the afternoon, there'll be drill, or arms drill,
or Ways of Using your Bayonet (with route march, or assault
    course

—*"The-only-object-of-this-is-to-make-you-HATE me!!!!!!"*—
still to come).

                    But now it's NAAFI break.
There's warmth in the Nissen hut; a girl will hand you tea,
you can count the rings on her fingers, choose your cake,

skim through the *Mirror*, day-dream of breasts, or faces,
re-light your crushed cigarette, have thoughts of leave
and when you'll ever get it; imagine new places,
and being there; or talk to Mike, or Doug, or Steve

of a far-fetched world of random odds and ends
where "Order Rules, OK"; where men have wives,
do jobs, walk dogs, skive off, mend cars at week-ends,
save for a semi-, and know what to do with their lives.

There will be nothing purer than this moment, now or later—
no pain-ceased wondering, no lawless murmurings of delight,
no consummation more than this, no happiness greater.
You knew it then for certain; and you were right.

NO CALL

"What's for fuckin' breakfast then, Dai?" "Fuck knows…
Fuckin' fuck on fuck…" Your day begins.
You make a bed-corner for Billy, lend socks to Steve,
hand Chris his letters. The barrack-time hooter goes
and we are there, heads bowed, shining boots. All except Wilkins
who "fell from the Menai Bridge" on his 48-hour leave.

24 across. Fight a war or learn a trade…
or slowly unravel… Give up the crossword (*A rope
ends it—anag.*) and take ten minutes reading.
Get your boots on; check the time. Four minutes till parade.
You can scan the hills from the doorway: there are some signs
        of hope—
three farmers on horseback, a girl with a ponytail walking.

For Blake, the tigers of wrath will always be wiser:
stay calm; keep your head down, wait for the time to go.
No call for doom-sayings, or higher things like courage
("Who speaks of victory? To endure is all," says Rilke).
You ruminate, and wait and wait. At dawn tomorrow
you will drive eighty miles and fire the guns at Sennybridge.

B-TROOP

A degree in maths might have helped. "Correction of the Day,"
wind charts, slide-rules, log tables, maps of the terrain,
OP reports—all combined (again and again)
to make four 25-pounders point the right way.

B-Troop, "officer material," we learned our parts:
don't get VD; take care when choosing your friends;
prefer gin and tonic; wear a hat at week-ends;
believe in the Empire (ignore what you know in your hearts).

There was never much sense of who we were—except once,
when the Colonel said "*You gents are lucky to be here.*"
Or—daily—as we lurched from the barrack-room, caps aslant,
"*chattering like monkeys,*" and the A-Troop bombardier
roused his men to their parade-ground-shattering chant:
"*What are they then, boys…???*" … "*ED-U-CA-TED CUNTS…!!!*"

ORIENTALISM

Quo fas et gloria ducunt

Her Majesty's Troopship Empire Pride had a holiday-mood
    white exterior
and a crew of black "Lascars" safely under her lower deck.
Out-bound for colonial Singapore—or if the gods willed, Pusan—
she cruised into an unknown zone between idleness and death.
The Atlantic brought wide horizons; there were apes on Gibraltar;
to the Port Said hypnotist your mind was "like a game of chess."
The Red Sea was flying-fish that could never be caught,
Aden an image of escape: an enfolding strangeness—
the work-smells of early morning in a foreign seaport.
Colombo had masks and devils and a religious wild-man.

The ship delivered us; we camped. Seven long weeks later
on the night-road to Changi the lights of a big cat's eyes
looked world-tired and ordinary. The six-foot venomous snake
curled like fire-hose on your bed was barely a surprise.
Prepared for death, not life, you were an impaired learner.
A concerned Buddhist on the sidewalk found words for you; knew
"All Westerners grasp at happiness"; that "Less may be more";
that "You will live to an age of not quite a hundred and two."
Unkind revelations; and final. So much for war.
This was a game that would need to be played for much higher
    stakes.

"ANY WONNY JINK?"

"Jink?" "Jink?" "Jink?" The wonny-jink boy slopes by
 clinking Coke and Fanta in his shoulder-basket. He solicits
        your eye
and would do anything to share your income, your job-tenure,
your escape from his hell-hole village, your so-perfect future.
Storm-shot, restless, indecisive—too thundery to eat—
the day drags out to its end. In this war-charged heat
it takes strength and purpose to laze a whole day through.
(He sells fans as well, and could even make your lunch for you.)

Ten miles inland, on a raked parade-ground in a lychee orchard
 the trucks are marked "Beyond Local Repair" and look newly
        battered.
All supply-lines are stretched for this scrap of Empire
and the phone-links to civilization have been re-classified "dire".
This is Goon-See transit-station: junk-town and half-way
        resting-place
 for deafened Grice, war-broken Callan, and Dicky de
        Mountjoy-Grace
 ("Profession: Poet and dreamer", though it is fifteen months
        since he has written a poem).
They drink Tiger, play five-card stud, and await the next plane home.

You will not be departing with them. In a recess of shade
        where rats scavenge
the gnats have assembled, and Battery Sergeant-Major Lowbridge,
Imjin River hero, and "inspiration for all his men",
 sits paring his nails—and muttering "Bastards........." again
        and again.
He grins, makes space for you, offers you a smoke—and
        brushes ash from your sleeve.
Another two months at the front and he could be home on leave.
 His eyes patrol the horizon. He clears his throat, and very
        quietly hums
"If you're ever... in a jam... here I am..." A useful thought for
        when your crunch comes.

CIVILIZATION

Colonel Tom Carey, Wagner-lover and C.O. of 14th Field
     Regiment Royal Artillery
had strong nerves, could sleep almost anywhere, but was
     doubtful about the army as a career.
Reluctant to dictate letters or to park his jeep with the hand-
     brake on
he out-manoeuvred surprises and saw beyond all particular
     locations. Self-dismissingly
he had accepted all foreign postings, gone where the army had gone
only to find himself and his distinguished regiment in Korea.

A month after supporting the Gloucesters on the Imjin
(deaths, shell-shock, invalidings home) he gave us his much-
     reflected-on view of the war.
It was civilization *versus* the faceless hordes. "Fifty years from
     now they'll be all over us unless we get ourselves sorted
     out first.
At least with the Germans you had common ground and you
     could imagine an end to it all." He once called us in,
poured sherry for the dullest of us, and explained that the
     National Service officers were better than the ones from
     Sandhurst:
(1) They knew how to lay the guns properly, and (2) "If you're
     fighting a war you don't want to be pig-bloody-ignorant
     about what you're fighting it for."

"How's the poetry going, Colin?" he even once wondered.
     Setting aside my airs and graces
he offered me his battle-scratched LP of Beethoven's Fifth.
     "As I'm sure you know...
I'd give you something much better but it's all I've got out
     here." He asked if I knew Strauss's "Four Last Songs,"
and this somehow led on to Shakespeare's thoughts about age,
     beauty and remote, not-quite-reachable mythic places.

Next time some of us had leave, he said, he would show us
round the best parts of old Hong Kong.
Off-duty, he would read Balzac into the night and listen to
Patti Page on the Forces' Radio.

II

LISTEN

Listen… Beyond the newscasts and the traffic noise:
from world-wearied Venice, forgotten Mantua, resigned Arezzo—
calm-bearing, transcendent, the far-off voices of boys
call to us down the centuries.
High-refined Palestrina, Monteverdi's rich certainties
sounding-out our daily lives, the sweet discords of Gesualdo.

Music for our grand despairs, for our still-believed-in dreams,
awakening us, reassuring us, telling us—
caringly, patiently, and yet again, on those days when it seems
that we are lost, all of us, and that there is nowhere to go
but onwards, downwards—what in our hearts we already know…
Only a god can save us.

LETTER TO A YOUNG POET

The fall of a girl's hair, the flare of a skirt—
the merciless daily things that break your heart
are there for you to learn your skills from. The hurt
of living is what stings us into art.

Cool your desires to ice, then start to play.
Compose it all like music: use what you need:
secrets; strange worlds; failed love; friends gone away.
Each poem's a rock-hard crystal, grown from a seed.

Dig down and find the past: dead kings; old war;
wonder-filled days; riding your first steam train;
mysteries; why men don't whistle any more.
Honour the things that won't come back again.

Remember politics, but don't digest them whole.
(That shimmering emblem trailed across the sky
will ravel out your mind, destroy your soul
and fill the world with lies while millions die.)

Be sure of nothing: youth's no time to be wise.
The Truth will let you in on its own plan.
Travel: possess the girl: enjoy each prize.
Don't think too much about writing. Live while you can.

STEAM DAY

It's something that seems remote from women's thoughts,
this ritual here today. "The Romance of Steam,"
fired-up once more: dark smoke, loud noise—lost days
when trains soared through the night, when the great Pacifics
toiled over Grayrigg, or trundling 0-6-0s
clanked between orchards to villages; an age-dimmed dream

re-fuelled to brightness. Brought here by neat electrics,
or on car-choked A-roads, noticing all the changes—seeing
the sheds-become-supermarkets, the bridge-piers that connect
nothing with nothing, the abandoned permanent ways—
they've come, in scores, untried, or all-but-wrecked,
summoned by a voice they've heard: the call of being

here for September Steam Day. Make no mistake—
some kind of God lives here. How else explain,
lured by displays of Walschaerts-gears and ports
(mothers-and-daughters preening, giggling, agreeing),
these grave-quiet boys; these old men—trying to make
a damped-down, off-track childhood right again.

OVERGROUND LINE

It runs through some built-up suburbs, past the back of everything,
through the wild woods of a rank, unrecorded countryside.
You see glimpses of roof-tops, a factory gateway, an open space,
but all round you, both sides of the line, embankment or cutting,
the plant world encroaches: you are in a miles-long secret chasm,
a valley of leaves and flowers that is its own place.

At the stations, grim-faced and paint-bespattered, still hanging on,
there are some signs of surrender: the grass-choked Victorian
platformsseem tactically half-abandoned, awaiting the axe.
In the long world between, there is calmness—all urgencies gone.
(The writ of this kingdom is absolute: contentment reigns.
Trains can go by, but must always keep to their tracks.)

This is our last unofficial paradise. If you stopped off here
you could lose yourself in this No-man's-land for hours.
Voices would call from the woods, the rabbits would speak to you,
there'd be an old caterpillar with his hat fallen over one ear.
Just count up to three and wish: bright stars of convolvulus
shine from the undergrowth, all fairylike and white and new.

The rest is purple—purple towering high over purple, at this
    time of year:
there's bellflower, hemp agrimony, mallow escaped from gardens,
loosestrife, woody nightshade, rosebay willow-herb with its
    feathery seeds.
You could dream new paths beyond everything, if you stopped
    off here.
In July's high summer this is thistle-and-buddleia heaven. You
    could walk back into your childhood
down a tree-high avenue of triumphant purple weeds.

LEWIS CARROLL'S "ALICE AS A BEGGAR CHILD"

He has penned her against a moss-grown wall. A soft light comes
hesitantly to the withdrawn garden, and her clothes, which do
    not seem to be her own,
are disarrayed, and have not been mended of late.
She waits, left hand on her hip—they have rehearsed all this
    charm—
her skirt in shreds, her right hand delicately cupped, pretending
    to beg,
an artfully-ripped sleeve half-dropped down her arm.
The sun caresses her face; it's 1858,
and you can almost hear the far-off wood-pigeons moan.
She holds it, head finely tilted; one sturdy leg
deranges a bed of nasturtiums.

She has put up with the tripods, with the being-arranged, with
    the benign photographer.
Her riveting dark eyes
see through you and her whole century.
Ready as she may ever need to be—six going on sixteen—
this too-composed waif, this far-too-precocious "beggar maid"
is familiar with the world's ways. Disdainful as a Queen,
she awaits the shutter—prepared for whatever it may be,
for the next needed pose. Nothing will come as a surprise:
she has discountenanced us—vamp or victim, waiting to be paid,
just as the photographer wanted her.

Like a dreamed-of fairy—or Donatello's David's sister—
she has reserved all her deepest secrets especially for you:
these rags, this too-dark hair, these exposed shoulders like sun-
    warmed pearls
are not her whole story.

                But enough of the camera's tricks:
despite so much beauty, despite the photographer's dutiful ways,
this is our best surviving photo.—No more pix,

and we must wish her well: one of the parade of girls
groomed up for marriage to Greek-reading whiskery husbands.
    Before she was quite through
she'd been a wife and a mother of three—but she remembered
    Uncle Charles. "Those Oxford days
were the happiest in all my life."

                    And he wrote his books for her.

THE GREEN PARROTS

They have come here from Asia
and flash through our garden with an easy beat of their wings.
One only, magical and uncalled-for, or in fours and in fives,
they congregate from nowhere and decorate our days.
Not "summer visitors," they have have been multiplying their
    numbers and are unfolding their lives
(eight hundred were seen last winter in a churchyard at Esher).
They live on seeds that they find here, do parrot-like things,
and do not care about our ways.

Like the darting swifts, gone by late July
(and who have never much noticed us anyway), they tease us
    with their grace
but keep themselves to themselves. When they sail through our
    different air
their in-flight callings are like a chattering of foreign words.
They build their homes in our trees, are well-groomed and
    beautiful, but belong elsewhere.
What future can there be here for psittacula krameri?
With tails like these, how will they learn to fit in here, to win
    their place
in The Nonesuch Book of British Birds?

It is a deep-down difference that nothing alters.
I would rather see them fanned against a tropic sky
or squabbling among junipers, their eyes like coal-bright gems,
or winging across the Irrawaddy with proper abandon
than gathered round all these sports grounds near Walton-on-
    Thames.
There are things that are only what they are in the places that
    they come from.
                As the summer falters
I think of our Christmas robin, imagine the next ice age, or the
    end of history; find myself wondering why
the friendly sparrows have all disappeared from London.

GREEN PARROTS 2

The ring-necked parakeet *psittacula krameri*, Britain's immigrant parrot, is now officially a pest.

What does being a pest mean? It means that you are no longer welcomed and can be shot.

These 16-inch-long bright-green birds are now the subjects of a "general licence" to kill, and have the same status as magpies, feral pigeons and crows.

What problems do the parakeets cause? They reproduce alarmingly and oust the native species from their roosts.

Aggressive to other birds and highly sociable among their own kind, they live in large colonies, and often beat woodpeckers and nuthatches to the best trees and nesting holes.

Once in place, the parakeets have few predators—they are a tough proposition for a house cat—and can outcompete local rivals forberries and seeds.

They can also be a threat to crops. Painshill Park vineyard, near Cobham in Surrey, claims to have lost enough grapes in a single day of parakeet visits to make 3,000 bottles of wine.

One of the most long-established of the parakeet colonies is now several thousand strong and lives in the trees around Esher Rugby Club, also in Surrey.

Since they are such "brilliant migrants," their numbers in Britain are increasing by 30% a year.

Does everyone believe that the parakeets are pests?

The London Wildlife Trust claims that they are "as British as curry" and that there is little evidence that they cause serious trouble.

A study from Sheffield Hallam University questions the merit of controlling invasive species at all. Most of "British" wildlife is a mix of the indigenous and the newly-arrived, and "eco-xenophobia" ignores most of the problems caused by native wildlife (brackendestroys heathland, badgers spread lethal disease).

Animal Aid points out that invasive species have become
	scapegoats for human failings (modern farming, urban sprawl,
	industrial pollution), and The Botanical Society for the British
	Isles notes that rhododendrons (Nepal) and the Corsican
	pine (Corsica) are among our most treasured species.
Almost the entire flora and fauna of the UK has arrived here
	since the last Ice Age 10,000 years ago. Some species have
	adapted more readily than others.

AMERICA

These rocks hurled at your defended train are a warning.
Another night, and it will not be boys, but men:
There will be strange lights, and the quick sounds of gunfire.
Many in your foremost carriages will die.
The wires will be cut: everything will begin to change.
It will be a new morning.

Five centuries of science and treachery have cut us off from
     our sky.
Everything must be turned around. Chile and Argentina
Will be saved from their greed, Mexico freed from its stasis,
The murderous power to the north where the earth's scum has
     gathered
Isolated like a disease.
A new basis will be found.

It will take us another five centuries
But we shall live simply; our numbers will be controlled;
There will be system and order on our way to the new age. Time
     will be on our side.
There will be an end to the lies, to the long compromise.
We shall stay strong, and nourish our rage; the other ways have
     been tried.
Blood will be shed, as of old.

We shall know what to do.
Not Montezuma, nor Atahualpa, nor Fidel, nor Che
Can be our guides along the paths of strife and to the sun-
     bright day.
Only the unborn can show us how a world must be forgotten to
     be made new.
Death will make space for fresh life,
As in the old way.

From the wastes of the north to the empire of the sun,
From the plains of the Dakota to the southern pampas,
America is uncovering its soul. A vision has been seen.
The forests will survive and flourish: the rivers will recover: the
     people will live.
The skies will be honored: the condor will pass.
Everything will be picked clean.

11TH SEPTEMBER 2001

It scarcely matters who conjured it, that September,
in the name of what God, or gods, or (with precision) why.
History has not yet ended: it holds its patterns,
and we still have leave to learn from them. Only remember

the night parades at Nuremberg, the dizzying lure
of every marching band—the rivers of torchlight,
the sudden sunlit flash of a girl's thigh,
the yearned-for loss of control, the forbidden rapture.

Two blooms of fire—and then, malignant elves,
bin Laden, in his rocky desert with nothing to hide,
showing with his hands to a friend the perfect beauty of it:
the monstrous towers, collapsing clean through themselves.

When Alaric camped his armies all around Rome
the Romans took two long years to believe that it was over.
Hitler spent hours communing with his model of Linz—
his thousand-year city—as the Russians' bolt slid home.

We live and die in dreams. Half-freed from nature
we are falling clean through ourselves. Dark gods prepare
and we slave to serve them, while poor democracy with its
        hands tied
degrades and fattens—brief window on a future.

EAST-BERLINER TRIES TO BREAK
THROUGH SECTOR-CROSSING-POINT 1985

A daring escape-attempt by an unknown young man at the frontier-barrier of the East-Berlin sector-crossing-point in Heinrich-Heine-Straße early Friday morning sadly miscarried. Driving a heavy building-vehicle, the refugee aimed to break his way through into the upper-Kreuzberg district of West Berlin, but crashed instead with his tipper-truck against a concrete road-block only a few metres before reaching the free part of the city. Frontier-guards immediately arrested him at gun-point and led him away.

This is how the failed break-out-attempt took place. Shortly after four in the morning a loud crash and the noise of an alarm-siren tore the residents of the West-Berlin side of the wall out of their sleep. From their apartments they could observe the closing-part of a drama which must presumably have had its origin somewhere in the vicinity of the Jannowitz bridge. From this direction, that is to say, the driver must have raced with his vehicle at great speed down the empty street towards the inter-zonal sector-crossing-point.

The blue tipper-truck had been equipped at its front end with a large earth-shovel. The vehicle shattered the first of the metal road-barriers like a matchstick. The second of the barriers was already open. After a hundred meters or so, the refugee came to the "slalom-stretch" of his whole escape-attempt. This was where he also met his downfall. A giant concrete-block stood in his way, and at the speed at which he was travelling he was unable to negotiate the sharp curve which faced him in order to drive around it. He trod instead on his brakes, and unavoidably crashed into the concrete obstacle. Three frontier-guards were at once on the spot, and with raised machine-pistols forced him to get down from the badly-smashed-in cab of his vehicle.

An eye-witness said: "With his hands on his head, the man in his dark working-uniform was made to go to a garage-building in the rear part of the frontier-station. There, the soldiers remained waiting with their automatic weapons continuously pointed at him. An hour or so later, the unknown man was taken away by uniformed *Volkspolizei*, once again in the direction of the Jannowitz bridge. No shots were fired during the escape-attempt, and shortly afterwards some military engineers arrived to remove all traces of the flight and to repair the damage to the wall."

Unnamed sources have today reported to this newspaper that the man's girl-friend lives in West Berlin.

ROAD

I drive across parallels,
Past equatorial jungles and dirt-blown intersections
Where hens scratch at roadsides.

The road encloses me, skirting the hot life
Of disease and villages, vultures on rooftops,
And girls wearing clothes.

                        These are places
To live and die in: to not become famous:
To pass out of reach.

A world's music blares from my radio.

As I step from the car at each border post,
My passport brings back to me
Who it is that I am supposed to be.

A POND ON THE HEATH

Five swans patrol the lakeside sun;
The young ones (grey) thrust out their heads
And stretch their wings.
Some leaves fall, circling, one by one,
On mist-damp seats. An old man sits,
Remembering things.

September days. But now, quite soon,
Time will surprise us: earth contrive
Its change of scene;
These hazy mornings, here since June,
Gather their skirts up; storms arrive
To make things clean.

The heath is closing down, it seems.
The trees go brown, will soon be bare—
As winds dictate.
Watch: as our year's last sun-warmed dreams
Go down to winter dark.
      Elsewhere,
The hot roads wait.

OCTOBER

October comes: the year resigns.
The currents down life's widening stream
run faster now. Like unpaid fines
the leaves pile up. Dark evenings seem
drawn out and under-loaded: lines
from poems that won't come right: a dream
of emptier nights. Encoded signs
for endings rather more extreme.

SNOWMAN

A great big smile, some mop-head hair,
a woolly scarf, wide trusting eyes,
protuberant carrot nose, a pair
of grandma-knitted gloves, large size.

Insignia of domestic bliss
were never more exposed than this.
All round our new-built snowman go
the fox's footprints in the snow.

CASE

Loving her takes its hold—and the slow dawning
that powers from some dangerous realm you can't define
are staking out their claim. You wake one morning
thinking of casual things—ancestral sign
the virus, far from gone, has plans to stay.
Slowly, her name, her hair, her voice on the phone
(upper East side) invade your starting day:
guests from a world more precious than your own.
You tell yourself she's not your type; or how—
"ten times her age"—you must be bad for her:
girl-driven self-deceits that make it plain
your judgement's failed you too: that nothing now
will halt the storm, or stem or stop the slaughter—
or wipe this out; or be the same again.

FASHION NOTE

They parade through your classier streets. Below the mini-skirts
their legs are an art-work, in tights that are sheer or not-so-sheer,
and their waists invite you. There's a mauled-schoolgirl look to
  their hair
but their heels are reckless (and we are in a bad recession this year).

Mostly they're blonde, but this is an opening statement only:
their dark-displayed roots speak a language you may need to learn.
They are on their way to somewhere, but are walking past for you—
they feel you watch them, and flaunt something at every turn.

And how beautiful they are. But there is only one way
  backward from here,
and they are taking it. Their kohl-deep eyes will weigh down
  your day
with the shadows of long-past wars: we are in a free-fall world now.
Black has become mainstream, innocence a card we play.

PEACE IN EAST SUSSEX

These old joiners'-wood trees, beech and oak and ash,
have stood their ground here for centuries. Through weather-
    lore's "soak and splash"
they have survived the seasons and foretold each coming summer,
friends to St Swithin and to changing cloud-formations.
Through reforms and persecutions they have escaped all axe-
wielders, their forebears witness to dancing-plagues and mass
    hysterias.

This early-summer breeze, fresh from the invasion coast
of Viking, Dane and Norman, seems hesitant, deferential almost:
there have been houses here for a thousand years, and there are
    new ones still.
Can this be England—unburdened now, shorn of her empire,
gathering her strength here?—enduring, safe as of old,
not part of the Europe where wars have rolled.

There are seventeen names on this lichened memorial. Lives
go on, plan their futures, expire in these wistaria'd drives
and have turned their backs on history. It will be a peaceful evening.
No storm-troops will visit, no books be read, or burned; no
    cattle-trucks arrive.
The sun will go down behind these clouded hills as always. A
    butterfly flutters by.

WORLD

"when the two-footed
Mammal, being someways one of the nobler animals, regains
The dignity of room, the value of rareness"
– Robinson Jeffers

Spengler was wrong: the world has *become* the West.
Japan has bowed out now; in China they buy art, drink wine,
play late Rachmaninov, groom themselves for decline
in Prada or Bulgari, wonder which limousines are best.

Our hard-won vision fades: dead faiths are reborn;
circuses rule the airwaves; Darwin makes way.
While bearded prophets prognosticate, announce their day,
their raw congregations pray and exchange their porn.

Time to turn out the lights. Too late to rely
on gold, ammunition, canned food; to make plans to revive
old powers we have lost: they are lost. Our last wildness gone,
we drift to our ending.
                          Lovely world, unready to die
slow death by two billion iPhones, you can still contrive
your disabling cataclysm. Some will survive. Bring it on.

REUNION PHOTO

Are their lives over? Why would they choose to be here?
(And with each other?) They've come by train from "town",
or driven cross-country; they've drunk some pints of beer.
Lunch digested, will they try the Cresta Run?
Migrate to Ulan Bator?—or kill their wives,
or re-embrace their old, half-cherished sins
(pretty Mills has grown up now, and has two chins)
or out-bid the Bank of England? The day winds down.
The account is closing. They have done what they have done.

They sit there, obedient, assembled in their rows.
Life has already culled them. No sign of Grey
(murdered), or Bottrall (AIDS), or Hanks and Boase
(drowned in Manaos in 1987).
Death sidles in when no more life survives.
These gave up long ago: how else explain
those sidelong looks of guilt, or mental strain—
that sheep-faced grin, those done-for suits that say:
welcome to the losers' club, the fourth eleven...

LEFT

Who is there left that you can talk to? Days go by.
"Friendless, deserted" (*The Beggar's Opera?*)—left in the lurch
(what lurch?)—you languish. Time to make plans to die?
You box up some age-stained letters, set aside more stuff,
but your heart's not in it. Tomorrow will be soon enough.
Another of your thoughtless friends falls off the perch.

Those language-teachers, those sergeant-majors, those not-
        quite-wives—
how old they must all be now! And those types at school:
grumbling, frowning, living their boxed-up lives—
Mr Cartwright-Brown would be a hundred and thirty-nine.
All gone… Time to wait out our world's decline?
(Wait even longer and watch the planet cool…?)

Be serious. It's not a dress rehearsal, OK…
Tune out the anguish—those *ennuis* just for you.
Take on the clichés, seize the remaining day,
put nose to grindstone, con yet another part.
Your younger son reads history, learns to play Mozart—
well there's him for a start: his dreams might see us through.

BEATING RETREAT

The ritual of Beating Retreat as you will see it this evening
Is an amalgamation of at least three ceremonies.
Certain aspects of these have been extended for you in order to enhance their value
    as entertainment.
There is the nationally famous band with its drums, counter-
    marching, leopard-skins, and finesse.
There is the valetudinarian Canon struggling with his
    incontinence and no longer quite sure where he is.
There is the healthily sluttish co-educational activity gradually
    developing around the edges of the quad.

Not too many signs of God; but the spirit of Modern History
    has been making an appearance.
A pilot waiting for clearance on the Gatwick approach uses the
    old water-tower for a marker.
Parents ("there is an 'income bar,' above which your child may
    be ineligible")
Sit around among champagne and picnicware; girls talk to boys.
A t-shirt reads *Born-Again Pagan*; the *ankh* is neck-ornament of
    the year.
Whoever planted the sequoias should be pleased with them after
    most of a century.

The last march lifts bracingly into the June air: there is no
    going back.
For them, now, there is only the silver of the rails, the rush
    towards jobs or marriages, the obstructive dealings with a
    difficult case of a father.
For others, this benign dusk:
The buddleias—"almost a weed"—fragrant behind deserted
    platforms;
The lights of the stations not stopped in; white signs that mark
    each slight change of incline;
The lush greens darkening along the sides of the track.

HEIDEGGER EXPLAINS

"[A] hope, today, / of a thinking man's / coming / word / in the heart"
– Paul Celan ("Todtnauberg"), trans. Michael Hamburger

We are hoping also. The task for *Dasein* (which happens to be
human) is still to wait.

It was a hard and wounding trial. The long arraignments began
when I distinguished (they said) between a "good" and "bad"
    Nazism,
or spoke unwisely—the Party's spies were at my lectures—of
    "the inner greatness of National Socialism."
Must I explain this still? We are uprooted from the earth more
    and more.
All that is great and essential comes from a people who have a
    home.
History drops away, but the earth remains.

Now I am dead, though still reviled, they can see
that I have brought an end to philosophy. There are no more
    certainties.
    They are on their own with Being.
There is only poetry, and thinking, and practical life.
Our helping word was in the poems of Hölderlin: only a god
    can save us.
Belief will come again, or else nothing.

I brought the young to Todtnauberg,
spoke to them of the Party, of the hope for the spirit, of your
    arnica and eyebright. Blood and soil… We did not talk
    about the Jews.
Do they now forget that we do not *live* on this earth any more,
that cruelty is not unusual, that there have been other holocausts,
that their politics of "values" rests only on the shiftings of
    blind will?

Their technology (which I warned against) speaks bravely of
    infinitudes,
not of here, of home, or of dwelling. It lends a hand to all
    planned killings.

The wearied earth cannot bear very much humanity.

TO BLAKE AND NIETZSCHE

Mistrust the man with *gravitas*. He has the soul of a slave.

Maturity is over-rated, mostly by those who have never been children.

Tact. Complicity in another person's self-deceit.

The door was invented on the way to civilization. Savages live open-plan.

Be superstitious, but not too superstitious.

Is post-modern art a new kind of art? Only if the warning notices, trial excavations, earth-moving equipment, multi-coloured safety flags and NO THROUGH ROAD signs we encounter on a major highway are a new kind of road.

> The world changes,
> Enabling you to die.

Where is the religion of dance and play? The orientals mostly sit.

All truth is carnal. That Energy is from the Body is the true meaning of the Word made Flesh.

The deepest truth of the world is religion. Its only Scripture is poetry.

THE SNOW

The clocks go back. October counts our days.
Winter awaits us—deep-inscribed by this date
to compel, for higher beasts, their restless change of ways;
for others, to bring long sleep or to obliterate

lifetimes. This grinding east wind from Treblinka, Sobibór,
Majdanek, will not disturb the way things go.
The year comes round again, and here we are.
Living our lives out. Waiting for the promised snow.

WEEDS

A heron ponders in a swamp of doubtful origin.
Hours he will wait, as bullfrogs croak and the pond's dark life
    goes on.
Potatoes flower beautifully in the nearby fields
And patchworks of useful crops stretch away toward the horizon.
Bees work the blossoms in fresh-grown hedgerows, with
    industrious noises.
A sparrow drops worms into its fledgling's mouth;
The fledgling hops about, and learns to be a sparrow.
By some old wooden huts, a man and a restless boy
Pile hay on an ancient horse-cart—a scene from Brueghel.
Spring has come back to Auschwitz-Birkenau.

They brought them here, through this brick-built railhead tower
That suns itself now like a page in an architecture book.
In these blank untenanted caverns two million traveled to
There is a dust-filled silence. The mute signs lecture:
Halte Ordnung! Sei ehrlich! Ruhe im Block! There are none left to hear.
Their irrecoverable voices have merged with birdsong.
At the far-off edges of the camp, the fences rust and decay, and
    the world breaks in.
A loose-hung door knocks emptily.
The tall, black watch-towers stand guard, but must be
    creosoted each year;
It takes work to keep this strange museum alive.

All across Europe the wood-pigeon broods.
To move. To move. A new move …
The exposed barrack-chimneys shift their lines—and seem
Like boats at anchor. Beyond the camp, toward Ošwiecim,
The train-tracks ravel in a blaze of golden weeds:
Wild mustard, yellow daisies, bird's-foot trefoil—all hazed with
    blue:–

cornflowers and forget-me-nots.
All tracks have weeds between them.
Soon now, their seeds will be lifted on the summer wind
To wander into the cracks and fissures of our clean new world.

The kindest flowers. The best memorial.

NOTES

Leni's *Triumph*

1. Early Leni *"The Holy Mountain" Der heilige Berg*, dir. Arnold Fanck 1926. *"The White Hell of Piz Palü" Die weisse Hölle vom Piz Palü*, dir. Arnold Fanck and G.W. Pabst 1929.

2. Leni's *Blue Light "Blue Light" Das blaue Licht*, dir. Leni Riefenstahl 1932.

3. Leni's *Triumph "Triumph" Triumph des Willens*, dir. Leni Riefenstahl 1935. *"The Triumphs of Caesar"* A nine-panel mural by Andrea Mantegna (c1431–1506), part of the Royal Collection at Hampton Court Palace. "triumphant, certain, dreadful" I have borrowed this notion from David Thomson, *A Biographical Dictionary of Film* (NY: Knopf, 1994), pp. 633–34. "Wired-in worship: what has really always been there" I am grateful to Tony Noguera for leading me to this formulation.

5. Leni's *Olympia "Olympia" Olympia* (Part 1 *Fest der Völker*; Part 2 *Fest der Schönheit*), dir. Leni Riefenstahl 1938. "Cranes, tracking shots, close-ups, back—lighting, slow-motion" These techniques were all either invented or revolutionarilyenhanced by Riefenstahl. "'Politics is the highest art'" "Politics too is an art, perhaps the highest and most comprehensive art there is, and we who shape modern German policy feel ourselves in this to be artists who have been given the responsible task of forming, out of the raw material of the mass, the firm concrete structure of a people. It is not only the task of art and the artist to bring together, but beyond this it is their task to form, to give shape, to remove the diseased and create freedom for the healthy" (Joseph Goebbels, letter to Wilhelm Furtwängler, April 1933). "Beijing will do this again" The overall re-designer of Beijing for the Games of 2008 was Albert Speer, son of Hitler's architect Albert Speer who designed the Games of 1936.

NAAFI Break

"NAAFI" (pron. "Naffy") The Navy, Army and Air Force Institutes, an association that provides canteens etc. for British forces in the UK and abroad.

Orientalism

"*Quo fas et gloria ducunt*" Motto of the Royal Regiment of Artillery ("Where right and glory lead"). "'Lascars'" Sailors from the Indian subcontinent employed on European ships between the 16th and mid-20th centuries. "Pusan" Disembarkation port for UN forces in the Korean war. "Changi" Changi Airport is the main airport in Singapore.

Steam Day

"connect / nothing with nothing" There are many Eliot (and Auden and Lowell and Larkin and other) echoes in these poems and the poet can only be aware of the most blatant of them. Homage, satire etc. aside, perhaps we are at a point in poetic history where we can accept such alludings (as with Shakespeare or the Bible) rather than striving officiously to point or root them out. It is language that speaks *us*, etc., etc.

Green Parrots 2

Most of this poem's material comes from "Briefing" in *The Week* (London), 31 Oct. 2009, p. 13.

Reunion Photo

"out-bid the Bank of England" In September 1992 George Soros made $1.1 billion by short-selling sterling against the Bank of England's attempts to maintain its value.

To Blake and Nietzsche

"The world changes" This two-line poem was sent to CF by Leonard Webb (British playwright, 1930–1995) and surely deserves a wider audience. "the poets have only interpreted the world…" Cf. Karl Marx, 11th thesis on Feuerbach.